CURTIS INTERNATIONAL
PORTRAITS OF GREATNESS

•

General Editor
Enzo Orlandi

Text by
Mario Lepore

Translator
C. J. Richards

Published by
ARNOLDO MONDADORI EDITORE
and
THE CURTIS PUBLISHING COMPANY

THE
LIFE
&
TIMES
OF

GOYA

CURTIS BOOKS
A division of
The Curtis Publishing Company
Philadelphia • New York

CHILDHOOD
IN ARAGON

Fuendetodos, a poverty-stricken Spanish hamlet consisting of stone huts and dusty lanes clustered about the rockiest and most desolate of the hills of Aragon, lies a few kilometers from Saragossa. Little has changed there since 1746, when Francisco Goya y Lucientes was born. His father, José, a master gilder of Basque origin, was often unemployed; his mother, Gracia Lucientes, who came from a family of *hidalgos* (the petty nobility), had a small patrimony: the house where Francisco was born. When he was five years old, his family moved to Saragossa. Here the boy spent the remainder of his childhood.

When he was 13 or 14 he was apprenticed to José Luzan, a skilled and successful artist who worked chiefly for churches: he specialized in large canvases done in a rococo and somewhat provincial manner. He was still influenced by the Aragonese style of painting, which had by then outlived its magnificence and vigor. The boy began, as was the custom then, by grinding colors. Four years later, he began learning to draw and to compose a picture. His models were the works of his teacher, and reproductions of the great masters. Prints of the latter, which were then making the rounds of Europe, were the contemporary equivalent of present-day photographs and art books. His first job was probably painting a cupboard for the parish church of Fuendetodos.

In 1764 Francisco made an unsuccessful bid for a scholarship for study at the Royal Academy of San Fernando in Madrid. He tried again, still unsuccessfully, two years later. Among his judges was Francisco Bayeu, an Aragonese who had moved to Madrid in 1756. He was an admirer of Raphael Mengs, a Czech painter whose smooth and academic works were very much in fashion in Europe at that time. Bayeu had a solid reputation. Goya enrolled in his school; along with Luzan's and Mengs's, this influence is evident in Goya's early works. In 1773 the young artist married Josefa Bayeu, his teacher's sister. Unquestionably this connection with Bayeu helped Goya at the start of his painting career. Soon after, presumably to oblige Francisco Bayeu, Mengs asked Goya to work with him at the Royal Tapestry Factory, of which he was director. Goya's job was to draw cartoons, or sketches, to be copied by the weavers.

Opposite page, top: Josefa, Goya's wife, who was devoted to him. Despite his affairs, the painter felt a real affection and deep respect for her. She was a great help to him at the start of his career, securing for him the support of her influential brother, Francisco Bayeu.

Opposite, below: Portrait of Xavier Goya, *the painter's only surviving child, who was born in Madrid in 1784. The painting, done in 1805, possibly for Xavier's wedding, brings the youthful figure to life elegantly and with a surprisingly free brush. The whole picture is bathed*

in an aura of pre-Romanticism. Above: Portrait of Francisco Bayeu, *a rather stern character. The courtly touches may have been a concession to the master's taste. After his initial patronage, Bayeu sometimes opposed Goya openly, but the two finally made up their differences.*

Drawing and graphics were, for Goya, a means of expression as powerful as painting. In the detail (right) from the Dream of Lies and Inconstancy, *an obscurely symbolic picture, a two-faced woman is kissing him as he sleeps. One face is loving, the other indifferent. The etching belongs to the Caprichos series.*

In the Self-Portrait (*below*), the play of shadows is singularly effective, and the plastic treatment well ahead of his time; it is in sharp contrast to the portrait of Floridablanca (opposite page), in which concessions to Mengs's style are neutralized by Goya's superb technique. It was from Velásquez that he took the idea of putting himself in the painting.

EXPRESSING
A WAY OF LIFE

"Art," George Grappe wrote, "is for Goya only one way, among a thousand others, of living and expressing the life which consumes and burns him." Goya the artist and Goya the man must be considered as a single entity. As an artist, he continually searched his innermost being to find the means of expressing a forceful and creative imagination that could bring to light a new concept of the world and of life. As a man, he coupled a passionate temperament with an astonishing physical vitality. He was a mass of contradictions: open-minded, ironic, realistic, and at the same time irresolute, occasionally timid, certainly easily influenced by circumstances and by the people he came into contact with. Undoubtedly the poverty in which he lived during his early years left him with a nagging fear of being poor again. He was essentially a man of the people; he had their vigor and their eagerness to succeed. He also had the instinctive plebeian awareness of the distance between his condition and that of the aristocracy, an enormous difference in the Spain of that time. His genius allowed him to rise to a high position, but he was always afraid of losing it.

Goya's chief strength lay in his single-minded and uncompromising devotion to his art. It was seldom that worldly consideration or self-interest could deflect his brush. A comparison of the self-portrait of 1775 with the portrait of Count Floridablanca will make this point clearer. The intent face under the shade of the wide-brimmed hat is youthful and rugged. It shows that Goya has outgrown his wild youth, when his innocence and recklessness combined to earn him a knife in the back in Madrid, and persecution by the Inquisition in Saragossa. The face reveals strength of character added to his native obstinacy. The portrait of Floridablanca, painted in 1783, is done in an altogether different style. As Goya wanted to please his subject, for once he painted an idealized figure, surrounded by testimonials of his power. But the characterization is still strong and sure. An oval portrait of the king hangs on a wall above a clock; on the table are plans for a canal and standing behind the table, the count's secretary or architect. In the left corner, there is a side view of the artist himself, reduced in stature and in a humble, almost obsequious position: he holds up his picture for the inspection of Floridablanca, who does not even deign to look at it.

Mengs, director of the
Royal Tapestry Factory,
instructed his artists
to use Flemish scenes
of childhood, French scenes
of gallantry, and Venetian
landscapes by Tiepolo
and Longhi (examples
on this and opposite page)
as a starting point
for their sketches. They
were, however, to produce
cartoons that were entirely
Spanish in character. Goya
did 46 cartoons between 1775
and 1791. Above: The Picnic.
Right: The Swing, reminiscent of a painting by
Watteau. Opposite page:
Blind Man's Buff.

CARTOONS
FOR TAPESTRY

It was probably Francisco Bayeu who launched Goya on his cartoon painting career. He not only persuaded Mengs to hire his young brother-in-law to work for the Royal Tapestry Factory but also shared with Goya the experience he had himself acquired in this technique. At that time he exercised over the younger man the authority of a master over his pupil. In addition, Goya and his wife had left Saragossa for Madrid, and had gone to live with him and with his brothers. As head of the family, patron and teacher, Bayeu so overwhelmed Goya that the latter's first five cartoons for tapestry lacked all trace of the strength and individuality that would stamp most of his work as uniquely his. Although he was already considered the best painter of Saragossa, where his beautiful murals in the Charter-house of Aula Dei were greatly admired, these early cartoons are completely uninspired. But Goya was too Spanish, too close to the people, too vibrantly alive not to capture the joyous Iberian temperament in his cartoons. He shook off his feeling of inferiority to Bayeu and, as early as 1776, with *The Picnic*, let himself go. Yet he was not impervious to the influence of other artists, if he could learn anything useful from their styles. Thanks to the example of Tiepolo, for instance, his colors became warmer and richer; his work began to show great vitality, and he acquired a feeling for spaciousness and luminosity.

FOUR MONTHS
ON A CUPOLA

Goya often recalled scenes of his childhood and adolescence when he was doing cartoons and genre paintings. These show an extraordinarily evocative and poetic force, and are a fascinating mixture of joy and melancholy. Reality, either dramatic, as in the *Snow Storm*, or picturesque, as in the *Customs Officers*, is tinged with nostalgia; it has the savor of something seen and yet drawn from memory. The joyous pastoral tone of *Summer* or the *Grape Harvest* does not detract from their realism. Goya once said: "I have had three masters: Velásquez, Rembrandt, and nature."

Goya's technique in these works is not academic; one feels that the artist participates actively in the life he portrays. Swift brush strokes point up a soft, clear color, either bathed in full light or placed in contrast to strong tones with few shadows; now and then he allows a violent clash of colors. His technical ability made it easy for him to work fast. It took him only four months to paint a mural covering the dome of the Pilar Sanctuary, a surface of more than 100 square yards.

This happy pastoral scene (above)
shows peasants relaxing with
their families. The mood of this
early work is far removed from
the bitterness and pessimism
of Goya's later years. He
is still bemused by the
simple charm of life as he
thought it ought to be lived
by the lower classes. Although
he was already seriously
disturbed by some of the
things he saw, he was still
able to shut out a great deal
that was worrisome and
depressing. This optimistic
outlook did not last long.
Opposite page, above:
The Customs Officers;
directly above: Summer;
left: Grape Harvest;
right: The Snow Storm,
the most beautiful
of the 1786 cartoons.
Its luminosity and realism
marked a new step forward
for Goya, but it presented
great technical difficulties
for the weavers.

The Parasol (*below*)
*is the most famous of Goya's
cartoons for tapestry. Done
in 1777, it is reminiscent
of Velásquez and, in its
feeling of spaciousness,
of Tiepolo. In its breadth
of contour, in the movement
and rhythm of its composition,
in the splendor of its warm*
*and varied color, it is a highly
individual piece of work.* The
Meeting (*opposite page, left*):
*this is thought to be a picture
of the Duchess of Alba and the
painter himself. One of the most
modern aspects of Goya's art
is precisely this recurring
autobiographical note. Far right:*
The Lady and the Soldier.

AN AFFECTIONATE BUT UNFAITHFUL HUSBAND

Although Goya was an affectionate husband, he was not a faithful one. His way of life, his passionate and exuberant temperament and the moral tone of the period all encouraged him to enjoy himself. But it is almost certain that he had only one lasting, real love affair: with the Duchess of Alba It was undoubtedly a stormy and painful one. It followed a liaison with the Duchess of Osuna, surely a peaceful and uncomplicated one, since the lady remained Goya's friend and patron.

He had been appointed to the Academy of San Fernando in 1780. The academicians did not care much for his art, but the aristocracy did, showering him with favors and commissions. Some of the nobles became his friends. Goya was an interested spectator of all aspects of daily existence; his keen observations, especially of the lively and colorful life of Madrid, are recorded in his paintings. Strolling through the streets, he gleaned hundreds of episodes, savored them, and was inspired to make gay and brilliant pictures of them. They were often gallant scenes, animated and joyous. *The Lady and the Soldier* is an example of one of these, and is at the same time a lively and accurate record of the fashions of the period.

A STAB
IN THE BACK

It was probably because of a woman that Goya, when he was young and still unknown, was stabbed in the back. The guard who found him in a Madrid alley at daybreak thought he was dead. Later, in 1770, in order to escape from the Inquisition, which for some unknown reason was close on his trail, he was forced to flee first from Saragossa, then from Spain. He went to Rome. Here he got into trouble again, some say because of a girl. In any event, he returned to Saragossa in July, 1771; soon after, he painted his first fresco, for the basilica of Our Lady of the Pillar. Despite the religious character of the subject, the painting exudes the fascination with women that pervaded his life and much of his work. He did not always look kindly upon them; many of his pictures display an irony tinged with contempt. This was perhaps the natural reaction to his ill-fated love for the Duchess of Alba. *The Viper Woman*, a drawing from the *Mirrors* series, is a clear indication of his attitude: a beautiful woman looks at herself in a mirror that reflects not her image but that of a snake wound around the scythe of Death.

Right: The Flower Girls, *one of Goya's most beautiful cartoons for tapestry, was done in 1786. It is a perfect example of his mature style, a scene that catches with grace and charm the life of the people. Opposite page: a detail. Above: the Bordeaux Milkmaid, painted in 1827. It was his last masterpiece, done when he was 81. His genius here anticipated all modern painting up to Impressionism. The softness of the rhythmic curves, the mastery of execution, especially the details of the scarf, the luminous values, the relationship between background and figure all create a fascinating picture. Goya effectively uses the material of the maid's skirt, which is done in short brush strokes, to counterbalance with its dark mass the lightness and transparency of the blue sky. Upper left:* The Viper Woman.

Left: The Letter, *painted around 1811, with its great feeling of space, shows an expertly painted contrast of pictorial values. The duenna, in the shade of the parasol that she is opening, listens to the girl reading the love letter that she has just handed her young charge.*
Below, left: Better To Be Idle, *an engraving in the* Caprichos *series, with the same ironic overtones. Directly below:* Two of a Kind (*from the* Caprichos), *a biting criticism of fashions of the times, insofar as dress indicated corruption, arrogance, misery and superstition.*
El Pelele (*opposite page*), *one of the last cartoons for tapestry, is more serene in tone. But the popular game, played with a puppet, has an obvious symbolic message.*

THE MAJAS: PICTURESQUE AND BOLD

The word *maja* might be translated into modern American as "moll." In 18th-century Spain, the *maja* and her companion, the *majo*, corresponded somewhat to the 19th-century *apaches* of Paris. The *apache* was a particularly flamboyant type of hoodlum, belonging entirely to the underworld: the *majo* was a member of the common people. Furthermore, a *majo* could rub shoulders with a duchess—and often did. The *majeza* was a link between the aristocracy and the lower orders. A noblewoman could dress and behave like a *maja*, discarding modesty in favor of a picturesque boldness.

Majas on a Balcony, which dates from around 1811, is considered one of Goya's most beautiful paintings. It was typical of a fashion and a way of life in Madrid that continued despite horrors and oppression. Manet must have had this picture in mind when he painted the *Balcony*. The French master, who greatly admired Goya, gave an accurate picture of Parisian middle-class life in his painting. Goya's evokes, penetratingly and seductively, the life of the common people of Madrid. In style, the painting is very different from his cartoons. He had by now achieved an extraordinary skill in creating atmosphere and at the same time maintaining realism. The Franco-Spanish war was to provide him for many years with subjects that he painted with a high degree of drama. But the everyday life of the common people continued to fascinate him.

Opposite page, left: Good Advice, *detail from the 15th plate of the* Caprichos. *Next to it is a detail of the famous* Majas on a Balcony. *Center:* Maja and Companions, *one of the cartoons done for the Royal Tapestry Factory between 1776 and 1779, certainly the most typical one of that period. Goya's cartoons,* because of the difficulty of transferring them to tapestry work, often brought forth complaints from the weavers. *Below:* Manola (*detail*). *This synonym for* maja *was the name given to the women of the Lavapiés section of Madrid. They usually belonged to the lower middle class.*

Below: four portraits of women. From left to right: Portrait of the Singer Lorenza Correa; La Tirana, *detail of her face at bottom of page;* Portrait of the Marchesa de la Solana, *and, last,* Lady with a Fan. *Opposite page:* Portrait of Doña Isabel Cobos y Porcel. *Proud and pert in her pose, well centered in the* composition, *the model is strikingly alive. The light from above brings out, against the black mantilla and the dark background, the face with its velvety eyes, the delicate, rosy neck, and the snowy top of the bodice. She is an imperious beauty, blonde and white, and yet typically Iberian.*

A SHREWD UNDERSTANDING OF WOMEN

Women in every walk of life were featured prominently in Goya's portraits. It was not only beauty that attracted him; it was also the discovery of the real person behind it. He was never dazzled by the expensive clothes of his subjects, although they gave him an excuse to show off with the paint brush. He saw through the proud bearing of these aristocrats and revealed their innermost being. His portraits of them betrayed their pride or vulgarity, their shrewdness or foolishness, their sensuality and their vanity.

Goya endowed his painted ladies with the warmth of living flesh. In the *Lady with a Fan*, the treatment of the hands and arms, in their transparent half gloves, anticipates by a good 60 years the Impressionist movement. Another perceptive portrait is that of the famous actress La Tirana, a native of Seville. Goya admired her for her talent, which was considerable. This portrait was done in 1794. The actress posed several times for Goya, who captured her warm, plebeian charm. He was interested not only in actresses but in the theater as well. Some of his small paintings on subjects from the drama are eerie and magical.

Three bitingly satirical and symbolic drawings. Below: the Dream of Lies and Inconstancy, *a detail of which has been reproduced on another page. Bottom of page, left:* They Say Yes and Give Their Hand to the First Comer; *right:* What a Sacrifice! *Goya jeers at the marriage of convenience, much in vogue at the time, and at its consequences.*

SENSITIVE TO HUMAN FOLLY

With the passage of time, Goya became increasingly sensitive to the terrifying nature of the world in which he lived. The passions of mankind dismayed him, and he was horrified to think that he, too, was a man. He was deeply shaken by the fury the Franco-Spanish War unleashed. Savagery, corruption, misery, superstition, ignorance, folly and cowardice were monsters that haunted him constantly. They ruled the people, the clergy, the court, all of Spain. Even though his life continued to be successful in the accepted sense of the word—he was wealthy and respected—the spectacle of life frightened and shocked him. His heritage was an austere and deeply religious one even though he himself was neither. He hated evil and injustice from the deepest recesses of his soul, even while they stimulated his imagination.

Despite a serious illness that left him deaf, Goya continued to turn out pictures at a tremendous rate until, about 1819, he began the paintings that culminated in the murals of the Quinta del Sordo (as his country house was known). His graphic work ran parallel to his painting; it is prodigious in its strength and individuality, its versatility and technical perfection. He was familiar with all the methods in use at the time: engraving, etching, dry point, lithography. Goya issued his first engravings around 1778: three aquatints on a religious subject, the oldest of which is probably the *Flight into Egypt*. In engraving, as well as in painting, he was well ahead of his time.

Opposite page, above: Two Peasants Fighting, *a mural from the Quinta del Sordo. The strength of the composition, the intensity of color and light, and the violent dynamism of the lines all convey the bestiality of the two men, so engrossed in their fight that they do not realize they have already sunk knee deep into the mire.*

Left: None Can Part Us, *an etching from the* Caprichos. *This may be a barb directed against a marriage that is failing but cannot be dissolved.* Right: Flying Men, Flying Machines, *from the series of aquatints that Goya titled* Los Disparates (Stupidities), *done when he was also working on the "Black Paintings" of the Quinta del Sordo.* Los Disparates *appeared in 1864, under the title* Proverbs. *A hallucinating fantasy is dominant here; the lines of the drawing are thrown into relief by dense grays.*

Goya's reputation grew steadily. In 1780 he became a member of the Academy; he was later received at Court; he painted portraits that assured his fame. Having won, in 1784, a contest for a painting in the Church of San Francisco el Grande and having also become painter to the Royal Family of Charles IV, he became the most fashionable artist in Madrid. An aristocracy that was narrow, bigoted and vicious opened its doors to him. His art had a novelty that pleased. And Goya himself appealed to this society, even though he differed from it in so many respects. He was attractive to the ladies who, at night, their faces half concealed by their mantillas, glided furtively in the streets, mingling with the *majas*. Men also liked him. His flattering portraits gave them a heroic air, an aristocratic distinction that they did not really possess. Goya was also much in demand for portraits of children. He was particularly sensitive to their freshness and candor, and skilled in giving an impression of tender young flesh. For all these reasons he achieved success in a haughty, exclusive, greedy society that was unconsciously galloping to its ruin.

Opposite page, left: Dona Tadea Arias de Enriquez, *an elegant painting of a court lady, a perfect example of his mastery. Next to it:* La Marchesa di Villafranca Painting a Portrait of Her Husband. *This page, above, left:* the gay Madrid Fair, *an event in which every inhabitant of the capital took part. Above: detail from the romantic portrait of the* Count of Fernan-Nunez, 1803. *Left:* Family of the Duke of Osuna. *The delicacy of the bluish gray tone that is predominant in the canvas is harmoniously broken by the green clothes of the children at the left and by the Duke's habit of puce velvet bordered with pink and silver. The composition is a classic pyramidal one. Right: detail from another painting of the Duchess of Osuna.*

25

"GOYA PLACED HIS SEAL ON A WHOLE SECTION OF SPAIN"

"El Greco created the Toledo we know, but Goya placed his seal on a whole section of Spain which, without him, would not have existed, and which he immortalized," wrote Focillon. Goya's contribution to art and to the world is extraordinarily broad and varied. His work depicts all aspects of life, from the humblest to the proudest, with a skill that has rarely been equalled in the history of art. His technique, which ran the gamut from a classical attention to detail to an impressionistic treatment of the whole, was buoyed up by a great feeling for rhythm and space, and a love for color in all its variegated possibilities—from bright, contrasting splashes to muted, misty half-tones.

His portraits often displayed an astounding candor and realism. The most striking example is undoubtedly the family group of Charles IV. This official portrait unmasks 14 people whose physical repulsiveness is more

than matched by their nasty natures. But he could also paint gentle and spiritual characters, as in the murals of the Charterhouse of Aula Dei in Saragossa (1774), the frescoes on the cupola of the Basilica del Pilar in the same city (1771–72), and those in the Church of San Antonio de la Florida in Madrid (1798).

He could handle with equal ease, as shown by his cartoons for tapestry, subjects in a lighter vein: scenes from popular life that exude a rare gaiety, freedom and charm. He loved the people, and for a while their occupations and pastimes made him smile. But as he grew older and more aware, and the political situation continued to deteriorate, he was gradually filled with despair. His later works were virtually an indictment of mankind. Once, in one of the 82 engravings of *The Disasters of War*, which he did between 1808 and 1810, he wondered: "Do they belong to a different breed?"

The Washerwomen (*above*) *is perhaps the most beautiful cartoon for tapestry, in its conception and color, of the group that Goya did in 1780. He had already spent much time at the Court of Charles III, and had taken advantage of this opportunity to study the royal collections, especially the works of Velásquez. It was then that he began to do aquatints; he also started his first engravings, a series of 18 plates inspired by the paintings of Velásquez and Carreno de Miranda. Opposite page:* Brawl at Venta Nuova. *Left:* Do They Belong to a Different Breed?

Left: Blind Man with Guitar, *cartoon for tapestry done in 1778.* *Along with the* Crockery Vendor, *it is the most famous of the series done that year. The face of the blind man (second figure from the left) hints at later expressionism; the boldness of the whole work is extraordinary.* *Below:* Poor People at a Fountain; *bottom of page:* The Wounded Bricklayer.

29

Below: You Who Cannot Go On, *from the* Caprichos. *The theme was taken from a revolutionary caricature, which, despite rigorous censorship, found its way to Spain. It represents a peasant crushed by a nobleman and a priest. Here the Spanish peasants bear the weight of two well-fed donkeys: the aristocracy and the* clergy. *Bottom, right:* Dance of the Charlatans, *a bitter satire against those who profit from the misery of the poor. It belongs to a series,* The Disasters of War. *Opposite page:* Desperate with Fear Lest Honor Be Lost. *In this detail of plate No. 2 of the* Disparates, *the specter of fear looms before fleeing humanity.*

THE INQUISITION AS CRITIC

Goya's great series of etchings are the *Caprichos*, the *Disasters of War*, the *Tauromaquia* and the *Disparates*, in that order. The *Caprichos* were done over a period of three years, from 1793 to 1796. The Inquisition interfered with their publication. In the *Caprichos* Goya gave free play to his biting satiric wit and his taste for the grotesque. His techniques in etching and engraving mingled to give quick effects of chiaroscuro and solid masses. In the *Disasters*, 68 of the prints deal with the war; the other 14 have political or social overtones. In the latter, Goya's humanitarian and liberal sentiments are evident. This explains why the political and social etchings remained unpublished during the reign of Ferdinand VII. They were issued later, as were the scenes of execution by a firing squad. In these, the technique of engraving was allied with touches of dry point to produce a more primitive and crude form than in the *Caprichos*. For example, light masses stand out against a dark background.

The *Tauromaquia*, an enthusiastic pictorial history of bullfighting, was finished in 1815, and published soon after without interference from any quarter. The sharp realism of these etchings achieves intense dramatic effects of motion. The pictures display an extraordinary limpidity of form, feeling of spaciousness, and penetration. The *Disparates* were done in 1817 and 1818. The poetic and fantastic world they depict links them to the *Caprichos*. But they are closer to the *Disasters* in form and style, for they show clearly Rembrandt's influence in the play of lights and shadows.

THE PASSIONATE DUCHESS

Opposite page: Portrait of the Duchess of Alba, *1795. This striking painting, with its bold juxtaposition of colors, elegance, and skillful execution, still has something stiff and conventional about it. During the same year Goya painted small pictures on amusing subjects and small, informal portraits of the retinue of the duchess as well as the full-length portrait of the duke (detail, below right). Below, left: Portrait of the Duchess of Alba, 1797. Like the other one, it was done in Sanlucar, where the duchess had retired after the death of her husband. X-rays have revealed, under the painted sand, the inscription "Only Goya," which could have been added later. Goya gave the picture to his son in 1812.*

The Duchess of Osuna captivated Goya. A woman of ancient lineage and great wealth, she was subtle and witty, elegant rather than beautiful. Perhaps he was less attracted by her wealth and her cultivated ways than by her passion for bullfighting. This was a strong bond between the great lady and the painter. The Duchess of Osuna was succeeded by Maria del Pilar Teresa Cayetana, 13th Duchess of Alba, who was 10 years younger than her rival. She was a flighty, passionate, faithless *maja*. Her love affair with Goya left him deeply scarred. He had known the Alba family since 1786, but his love for Cayetana probably flowered between 1795 and 1797, the dates of the two portraits of the duchess. The difference between these two works suggests the change in their relationship. The first portrait is formal; Cayetana poses in a white dress with a high, prominent scarlet sash. The 1797 portrait creates a different impression: it is familiar, flirtatious. Cayetana, in her black mantilla and dark clothes relieved by splotches of color, stands out against a distant landscape and a blue sky. The slender little figure breathes spontaneity. On her right hand she displays two rings on which are inscribed Goya, Alba.

It is hard to say what attracted the youthful duchess, widowed for a year, to the painter, now close to 50 and deaf. Goya cannot have been an easy companion, but he was passionate and highly imaginative; perhaps she found him intriguing. Almost nothing is known about the course of their affair. Cayetana had the instincts of a *maja*, and he quite naturally took his place in the world of the *majeza*. He was to paint her in poses of the most abandoned intimacy. As a prelude to the portrait of 1797 there was an album of sketches and portraits of the duchess, all done at Sanlucar. In these drawings there is a feeling of joy and balance, but there is also a veiled hint of uncertainty and jealousy, and, in the last ones, an aura of general moral laxity. The *Caprichos* make readily clear, as these Sanlucar notebooks do not, how bitter the beautiful and inconstant duchess made the painter. An echo of her still sounds in the two famous paintings done around 1800, the *Clothed Maja* and the *Naked Maja*, although the duchess did not serve as model. When Cayetana died in 1802, Goya was torn with grief.

Goya was appointed first court painter in 1799, and the following year he painted the Clothed Maja *and the* Naked Maja (below). *Both paintings belonged to Godoy, the all-powerful minister of Charles IV. The paintings were said to have been placed one over the other in a room in his palace; they could easily be interchanged by means of a mechanical device. Opposite page: detail of the* Clothed Maja.

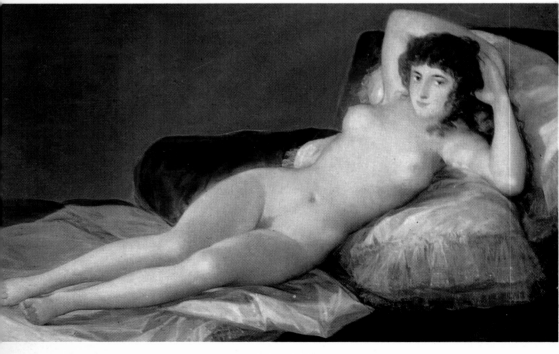

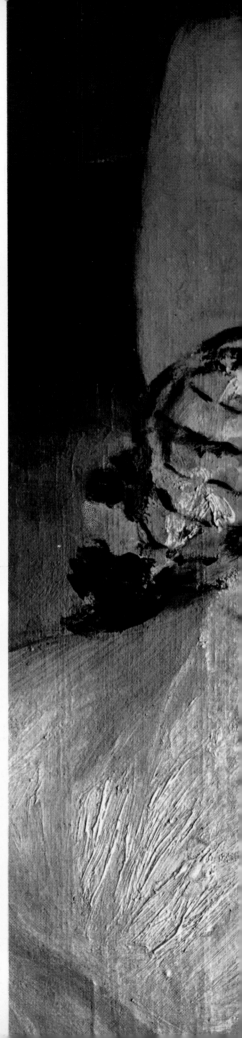

Below: The Game of Pelota, *cartoon for tapestry, 1779. Note how cleverly the artist holds together a rhythmic horizontal composition by enclosing it vertically between the cluster of trees and the almost geometric mass of the walls. The painter sought, above all, a pleasant feeling of movement, a beautiful decorative effect—essentials for a tapestry.*

Opposite page, above: Carnival Madness *from the* Disparates *or* Proverbs. *A bestial frenzy seems to have gripped the characters, whose faces are frightening. Goya's imagination grappled with the absurd, and he symbolized in a disquieting way the general lack of conscience. Right:* The Stiltwalkers, *another picture that captures a popular flavor.*

BREAD
AND CIRCUSES

There was less and less money from the American colonies; the French Revolution and then Napoleon set Europe in a turmoil; poor administration was ruining the nation; the Inquisition ruled; smugglers and bandits were becoming increasingly numerous. But none of this bothered a wealthy, frivolous, stupid aristocracy that was less and less able to discharge its duty of upholding the throne and the country. Nor was the situation of any interest to a clergy so rapacious that it pocketed perhaps one-third of the national income. Occasionally frightening news of changes in the world came from the outside, but this did not affect Spain internally.

Nor did the common people, downtrodden and poverty-stricken, pay much attention to what was happening. They lived from day to day, content with bread and bullfights. Theirs was a fatalistic acceptance of life in keeping with their capricious natures; it took very little to arouse in them a collective gaiety. And their masters were well aware of this. The motto "Feasts, Bread and Gallows" of Ferdinand II of Bourbon, King of Naples, was one suggestion for governing a kingdom, and his close relations on the Spanish throne followed it. Goya, who was still a man of the people, despite his efforts to ennoble his name, never lost his knack for portraying ordinary Spaniards in all their activities and pursuits. He was constantly worried about the future, yet he was attracted to the hand-to-mouth philosophy of the poor.

Above: The Family of Charles IV,
*a masterpiece of portraiture,
done in 1800. The characters
are arranged in two tight groups
on the right and on the left,
and a looser one in the center.
There is not much depth;
the light shines softly from
an invisible source, probably
facing the family, directed
from the left at an angle of
approximately 45°. From left to
right, they are Don Carlos Maria
Isidro, Goya himself (in shadow),
Prince Ferdinand, Doña Maria
Josefa, the fiancée of Don
Ferdinand (with her face averted
because no one knew who it was
to be), Doña Maria Isabel, the
Queen, Don Francisco de Paula, the
King, Don Antonio Pascual, Doña
Carlota Josquina, Don Luis de
Parma, and his wife Doña Maria
Luisa with her infant son Carlos
Luis in her arms. Right: detail of
the numerous glittering decorations
that cover the king's chest. Left:
another detail, of the central group.*

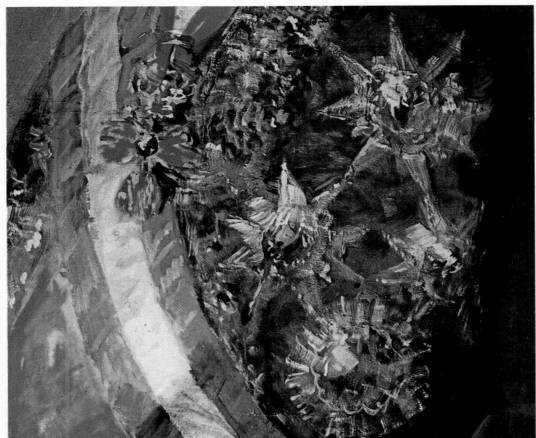

PITILESS
IN HIS PORTRAITS

Right: Detail of a Portrait of Godoy. Below: Queen Maria Luisa on Horseback. Goya did not always succeed in his paintings of animals: this horse was criticized, but there is something monumental about the painting. Opposite page, left: the head of the Queen, from the family portrait; next to it, another view of her in the Black Portrait.

The powerful, sharp and pitiless characterization of the face of the queen, as she appeared in ceremonial attire in the family portrait, found its counterpart both in the equestrian painting done the preceding year and in the black one with a mantilla done in September, 1799. Both portraits show the same woman: conceited, passionate, frankly homely. Perhaps in the black portrait there is a slight softening. Vanity, however, is blind: the queen was pleased with her likeness. The family portrait, in which all except the infants are treated as posturing monkeys, and in which she herself looks like a shrew, delighted her. The king also was quite happy to appear a rather stupid oaf surrounded by people who were later to provoke laughter and sarcasm. Charles IV never saw himself as Goya portrayed him, ruthlessly and pitilessly revealing his innermost being. The whole family was delighted by the skill with which Goya painted them. Not one of them really saw the overdressed puppets covered with medals and decorations. The aging queen had eyes only for her lover, the min-

ister Manuel Godoy. Even the king looked upon Godoy as his "best friend."

Godoy, a member of the minor nobility from Badajoz, had rapidly risen to a high position, with the queen's help. He controlled the destiny of Spain. In 1798, faced with the choice between an alliance with England and one with France, the minister played a dangerous game of seesaw; he finally offered Spanish mediation between France and the Vatican. At that point the Anglophile party, the Catholics, and his other enemies created such a crisis that he was obliged to retire from the scene. The king dismissed him with tears in his eyes. But after the 18 Brumaire, Charles IV became unexpectedly friendly with Napoleon, showered him with gifts and recalled Godoy. Napoleon made the minister a present of the tapestries he himself had been given by the Spanish king. This was in 1801. It was decided to declare war on Portugal in order to detach her from her alliance with the English. Godoy was promoted to the rank of general.

THE QUEEN'S LOVER— INDISPENSABLE TO THE KING

Manuel Godoy was a good customer of Goya's; he bought from him, among other things, the two famous paintings of the *Naked Maja* and the *Clothed Maja*. Godoy was dishonest and amoral, but he was also extremely attractive and likable. A brilliant man, he had just enough cultivation to impress the court and appeal to the ladies. He spoke French and Italian, knew a little Latin and Greek, and was versed in mathematics and philosophy. Destined from his earliest years for a military career, he was an accomplished horseman and a crack shot; he played the guitar well and often accompanied himself with it when he sang—in a pleasant voice—folk tunes and popular airs. The court was a boring place, and it is not surprising that with his talents and charm he should have quickly achieved success.

He was born in 1767; at 17 he went to Madrid to enter the Royal Bodyguard, where he soon came to the attention of Maria Luisa. The king, for his part, found the young soldier, who sang so easily and well, increasingly attractive. Godoy, a past master at livening things up, was soon very popular at court. His rise to power began in 1792; in 1795, when hostilities between France and Spain came to an end, the king gave Godoy the title of "Prince of the Peace"; two years later he gave him his own niece, the Countess of Chinchon, in marriage. The queen was not pleased by the event, but Godoy affected not to understand. He was often to make use of jealousy to keep Maria Luisa in thrall. His affair with a beautiful Andalusian, Josefa Tudo, known as "Pepa," drove the queen wild; a later one with the fickle Duchess of Alba gave rise to rumors, when Cayetana died in 1802, that Maria Luisa had had her poisoned to avenge herself on the minister. But Godoy always managed to make up with the queen and to remain indispensable to her husband.

When the Countess of Chinchon, whom Goya had already painted as a child, married Godoy, the painter did a portrait of her that is one of the most elegant, exquisite and sympathetic in his long gallery of portraits. The dark background against which the little figure sits sets off her delicate face; the tight composition, the fragility of the colors, the fineness of the brush strokes, and the balance of the whole are the work of a master.

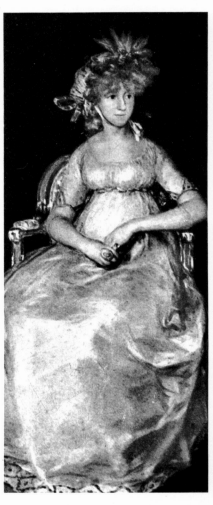

Top, *left:* The King's Safety Does Not Require Torture; *right:* If You Are Guilty, Die Quickly: *two aquatints in the* Three Prisoners *series. Goya lived through the tragedy of war-torn Spain without giving vent to any particularly patriotic protests; for him war was madness, whoever the participants might be. Below these*, Portrait of the Countess of Chinchon, *wife of the minister Godoy; the painting was done in 1800.*

58

Left: Thank You for the Meal *and, right:* What Good Is a Cup? *from the* Disasters of War. *Below,* Portrait of Manuel Godoy After the Battle of Narajas. *In his elegant uniform, with a saber by his side and the baton of a commander at his knee, the royal favorite poses in the "fires of war." Goya deliberately painted out any expression in his face.*

Goya was certainly not an admirer of Ferdinand VII. During the latter's exile in Valençay, he painted a portrait of King Joseph Bonaparte and his generals, and then one of Wellington (1812). Ferdinand said to him in 1814, after he had returned to his throne: "You deserve not only death, but hanging. If we forgive you, it is because

we admire you." Below, Equestrian Portrait of Ferdinand VII. It is remarkable for the splendor of the figure against the cloudy sky and the expert handling of technical problems. Opposite page: Portrait of Ferdinand VII in his Coronation Robes, another dressed-up puppet with a disagreeable face, thick eyebrows, a furtive look. When Goya painted, he paid no compliments.

PLOTS AND CONSPIRACIES

Ferdinand, Prince of Asturias, eldest living child of Charles IV and Maria Luisa and heir to the Spanish throne, was born in 1784. An unloved child, he hated his parents, whom he was later to betray. When the Peace of Amiens, drawn up in 1802 between England on the one hand and France, Spain and the Batavian Republic on the other, was broken in 1803, Ferdinand was 19 and ambitious. Soon Spain was torn between France, which exacted tributes from her, and England, which ruled the seas and repeatedly violated Spanish territorial waters. Godoy behaved with circumspection, but made some mistakes: the clergy hated him because his views seemed advanced, even liberal; the people hated him because he had forbidden bullfighting while the war was going on. Those enemies of the favorite rallied behind the heir to the throne. Godoy annoyed Napoleon and had to resign.

But he still held a trump card: he had accurate information on Ferdinand's plans. One day in October, 1807, Charles IV found on his work table at the Escorial a note that said, "A palace revolution is being planned right now. The throne is in peril, and Queen Maria Luisa is about to be poisoned." The king acted immediately: he sent for his son and dispatched a messenger to Godoy, who came promptly. The meeting between the king and Ferdinand was a stormy one. Godoy—who had planned everything—arrived in Madrid and was given carte blanche. The degrading affair petered out with the submission of Ferdinand, who betrayed his accomplices and was forgiven by his parents. On the eve of the French invasion, Ferdinand and his friends started the rumor that Godoy was planning to let the sovereigns flee to America to one of the colonies that Ferdinand himself was to lose later in his reign.

The news caused a popular uprising. The troops, called out by the prince, fired on the crowd; a massacre ensued. The king and queen begged their son to quell the revolt. Meantime, a few officers went to Aranjuez, where Godoy was living, discovered his hiding place in the palace and carried him away, covered with wounds, while the crowd looted the minister's magnificent residence. In March, 1808, Charles IV abdicated in favor of his son. Then it was Ferdinand's turn to abandon the throne. Joseph Bonaparte, brother of Napoleon, became King of Spain.

CONCERNED WITH HISTORY, NOT POLITICS

Opposite page: Executions of May 2, 1808. *The composition is rhythmically and plastically dynamic: the combatants form a tumultuous mass of brilliant colors, which are deliberately not highlighted because the artist wanted to create the illusion of movement. This painting obviously foreshadows Delacroix and the Romantic painters. Below, left:* The Execution of May Third; *right:* What Courage! *from the* Disasters of War. *Bottom of page: detail of the* May Third. *Whereas the firing squad is seen only from the back, as a brutish, anonymous mass, the patriots are shown from the front, their faces and figures detailed in a variety of expressions and attitudes. The focal point is the man in the white shirt, bathed in a clear light, who flings out his arms, offering himself as a target for the guns in a bold gesture of despair and sacrifice.*

After Charles IV and Ferdinand VII had gone into exile in France, the people rose up against the French invaders. It was a bloody war, with both sides committing atrocities. Whenever it seemed to die down in one sector, it would spring up anew in another. When the Duke of Wellington, applying the "scorched earth" policy, advanced with his army into the desolate Iberian peninsula, there was nothing left for the French to do but to retire. Goya's records of these events are gruesome, but they are among the best examples of his art.

His personal attitude was not patriotic. Living as he did the life of the court, he was well aware, despite his wealth and fame, of the effects of bad government in Spain. A liberal by instinct, a man of progressive ideas, receptive to the concepts of revolutionary France and what Napoleon originally stood for, he at first welcomed the invaders. But he was not entirely satisfied; what he observed of the horrors indulged in by both sides kept him neutral: there was nothing to choose between the French and the Spanish. He was on the side of humanity, reason, peace. It was an abstract position, but he was an individual who lived in an ideal world of his own, on whom deafness had imposed another barrier. He saw the future as well as the present; his art was concerned not with politics but with history.

On May 2, 1808, the people of Madrid rose up against the Mamelukes of Napoleon's cavalry. It was a bloody episode: armed with knives, clubs and stones, the people threw themselves against the well-armed and well-trained soldiery. It became a slaughter that continued on May 3. The nighttime executions, by firing squads, of rebellious patriots accounted for numerous additional victims. In 1814 Goya commemorated the Massacres of May 2 and May 3 in two outstanding paintings, masterpieces of historical evocation, great symphonies of violence and horror.

THE HORRORS OF WAR

Opposite page: General Don José Palafox on Horseback (*1814*). *This is the most imposing of Goya's portraits of the heroic defender of Saragossa. Below: detail of the portrait (1798) of Guillermandet, French Ambassador in Madrid. Bottom:* Portrait of Wellington. *This painting, stolen from London in 1961, was found in Birmingham in 1965.*

After the events of the second and third of May, 1808, quiet was restored in Madrid. Although Goya had witnessed events that had troubled him deeply, he remained friendly with the backers of the French, those who today would be considered "collaborationists." It seems almost certain that in that year, from October to December, he was in Saragossa. Here, on May 25, 1808, the people appointed José de Rebolledo, Count of Palafox, commander general of Aragon. Saragossa repulsed a first attack by the French. In February, 1809, after a savage siege and prodigies of valor, the city was forced to surrender. It was by then half in ruins. During the months he spent in Saragossa, Goya drew and painted episodes of the struggle. He later recalled it in a series of oil paintings; teeming with life, they forcefully and faithfully record events and disasters seen at first hand. Twelve of these paintings are known to have survived: they are called *The Horrors of War*. But a portion of his works, those painted in 1808, were in Palafox's studio. When the French finally captured the city, they were slashed and destroyed by French bayonets.

Once back in Madrid, Goya took up portrait painting again. As the king's First Painter of the Chamber—an office that he had kept—he painted the *Allegory of the City of Madrid*, which is in the city hall of the capital. The period from 1808 to 1812 was one of feverish artistic activity, although commissions were scarce.

In June, 1812, his wife died. She had always remained in the background, but she was an essential part of his life. The importance of Josefa Bayeu to her husband can be gauged by the amount of jewelry, furniture and paintings—Spanish and Italian as well as Goya's own—that figured in the inventory of her possessions. It also revealed an interesting picture of her private life. Josefa's death, as well as the Duchess of Alba's, was another of the blows that drove him to the desperate painting of the Quinta del Sordo.

On these two pages, four pictures from the Disasters of War. *Below, left:* There is No Remedy. *The theme of the firing squad is once more taken up with a tragic intensity of expression. The figure of the victim tied to the stake is highlighted. Below, center: detail of* For a Sword. *Below, right: detail of plate entitled* Unhappy Mother, *showing a child crying at her mother's terrible fate. Opposite page: detail of* They Don't Want It, *from the* Disasters of War. *Savagely attacked by one of Napoleon's soldiers, the woman wildly defends herself.*

NO HEROES— ONLY VICTIMS

Goya's eyewitness recording of the six anxious war-torn years through which Spain had just lived sounded one single, clear note: war is a catastrophe; it unleashes the bestiality of man; it causes suffering and degradation. He never recorded military events. In the *Disasters* and in his canvases there is not a single picture of a battle. There were never any heroes; if there was a protagonist it was always a victim. Yet, in the long run, he held responsible the victors and the vanquished alike. In his feeling of horror, in his raw presentation of victims and slaughter, he reveals an anguished compassion for man.

The events that he witnessed at such close range and with such intensity of emotion made him feel increasingly isolated. It was perhaps because of this that, when he painted for himself alone, he occasionally reverted to peaceful scenes of the everyday life of the people to whom he had always been attached: it was a form of escape for him.

CONTINUOUS ARTISTIC DEVELOPMENT

Goya's artistic development has been commonly divided into four phases. In fact, it was a continuous development, a progressive perfecting of his technique and an ever-growing breadth of concept. Every time he took up a theme whose possibilities seemed to have been exhausted, he managed to imbue it with renewed vigor. Once he had said that his masters were Velásquez, Rembrandt, and nature; but in his old age he discovered that color matters little; what counts is tone. He commented later on his own paintings, *The Executions of May Second* and *May Third*, which were of a frankly revolutionary nature: "I see masses, not lines, and my brush must not show more than I see." So it was Goya himself who provided the key to understanding his work. In a drawing he did when he was 82, shortly before his death (perhaps at the time of the *Bordeaux Milkmaid*), which shows an old man walking along supported by a crutch and a cane, he wrote: "I am learning, still learning."

AN ABYSS OF DESPAIR

The thunder of war had grown faint, but clouds remained on the horizon. They were not dispelled by Ferdinand VII's return from exile in Valençay. He abolished King Joseph's constitution of 1812, restored the Inquisition, recalled the Jesuits who had been expelled by his grandfather, and started reprisals against the collaborationists and the liberals. In 1820 he granted the people a constitution, but withdrew it three years later. Goya did several portraits of this faint-hearted tyrant who was bent on avenging past grudges and humiliations.

Goya was by this time in such great demand as a portrait painter that he was unable to accept all the commissions he was offered. But the peace that success and prosperity had given him before the war did not return. "The Deaf Don Paco," as his familiars called him, was secretly prey to an ever-increasing anxiety, which found its only expression in his paintings. The works of this period, in both subject and technique, were years ahead of their time. His need to cut himself off from the world around him had become so imperative that in February, 1819, he bought, in the country near Madrid, the house known as the Quinta del Sordo. After another serious illness, he retired to it the following June. There he sank into solitude as into an abyss of despair. Everything he had seen and done, all the thoughts that troubled him, all the anguish he had ever felt assailed him.

He translated his inner turmoil into paintings on the walls of his house. This ability to express himself may well have saved him from madness. His pessimism found its outlet in a frenzy of creativity—his nightmares and hallucinations, exorcised, covered the walls, leaving his soul at peace. A series of small paintings, done in a vein that was as cruel as it was fantastic, belongs to this period. It may be that some last sacred pictures were also done at this time: Saints Peter and Paul, now in an American collection. The pictures of the Quinta, acquired in 1873 by Baron Emil von Erlanger, were stripped from the walls where they had been painted and transferred to canvas. In 1882, Erlanger presented them to the Prado Museum in Madrid.

Below: Saturn Devouring His Son. *The painting belonged to the frenzied decoration of the dining room in the Quinta. It is the prototype of all "cruel" painting, a genre in which a long succession of artists from the Romantic period to the present have expressed horror. Below, right:* The Colossus, *at the Metropolitan Museum of Art. There is another treatment of this subject at the Prado (opposite page). This version is sometimes called* The Panic. *Some critics have related it to the dreadful nightmares from which the painter suffered between 1819 and 1828, and which undoubtedly inspired many of his murals. In the painting, panic-stricken hordes are fleeing before a giant; only a donkey remains stupidly indifferent.*

LAST DAYS IN FRANCE

As a strong supporter of the short-lived Constitution of 1820, Goya became suspect when Ferdinand VII re-established absolutism. The king withdrew his protection. At the beginning of this period, the painter found refuge for three months in the house of Don José de Duaso y Latre, a priest and editor of the paper *The Gazette.* Goya painted his portrait and that of his nephew, then returned to the Quinta. However, in constant fear of persecution, anticipating the worst—arrest or confiscation of property—he gave the Quinta to his grandson Mariano, and in 1824 asked leave to go to France to take a cure at the thermal baths of Plombières. Later he asked for an extension of his stay in France. In 1826 he returned to Madrid and was granted permission to retire.

In July of the same year he went to France again. His grandson accompanied him to Bordeaux. Here he painted, drew and etched. He worked fast and vigorously, creating for himself an entirely new style and color sense. The famous *Bordeaux Milkmaid* belongs to this period. His final style was rich with lyricism, controlled strength and bold modernity in composition and technique. But Goya did not develop this new style. He left that to the great painters of 19th-century France, from the Romantics to the Impressionists, who learned much from him.

Goya died on April 16, 1828; he was 82 years old. His remains did not reach their final resting place, in his native country, until 1919.

This self-portrait is the first
plate in the Caprichos, which
were put on sale in 1799.
There are a great many self-
portraits of Goya in existence.
Sometimes he put himself into a
group, as in the portrait
of Count Floridablanca and
the famous picture of the
Family of Charles IV. Among
the youthful self-portraits is
one, now in the Zurgena collection
in Madrid, that almost certainly
dates from 1774. It shows a man
with deep-set eyes, a high
forehead and a rather broad
face; altogether, a determined
and thoughtful face. In subsequent
portraits, the passage of time
and life itself have added to the
face a steadily more noticeable
melancholy. Sometimes he looks
frankly dramatic, as in the portrait
that now hangs in the Goya
Museum in Castres. This one
bears a slight resemblance to
the Beethoven of certain Romantic
prints. Here, the typical beaver
hat, long sideburns and cravat
create an impression of a man
who, without being a dandy,
is fashionably dressed. He has
great dignity, as befits an artist
now universally appreciated.
But in his eyes, on his lips, there
is something that conveys
a sense of isolation. Goya is
self-contained; deafness has
put a barrier between him
and the world. The knitting
of his thick, bushy brows,
the long lines at the corners
of his mouth, the slanting,
suspicious look of the eye all
reveal suffering and distrust.

Just as every great artist of the past belongs to the present too, so his work in turn makes its mark on the future. Goya belongs to this immortal company. He left to his followers a legacy of innovations that has not yet been exhausted. He was a poor teacher, so he had no pupils, only imitators. But later artists found in his works the seeds of most modern art. The themes of his work are still apposite: his indictment of human weakness, stupidity and cruelty is as pertinent today as it was in the Spain of the Inquisition and the decadent Bourbons. After a slow beginning, when he absorbed the essentials of the art of Velásquez, Rembrandt and Tiepolo, he resolutely turned his face to the future. At once realistic and visionary, crude and refined, plebeian and aristocratic, he conveyed the essence of life through his art and, by his painting and etching, helped bridge the gap between the 18th-century world and ours.

1746—March 30: born in Fuendetodos (Saragossa) to Francisco de Paula José and Doña Garcia Lucientes.

1760—Apprenticed to the painter José Luzan in Saragossa.

1764—Fails to win the contest sponsored by the Madrid Academy.

1766—Loses in the contest a second time.

1770—Goes to Italy, partly because of his lack of success with the Madrid Academy, partly because he wants to see Correggio's pictures, and especially because of troubles with the Inquisition. Places second in a contest sponsored by the Parma Academy. In some of his letters he proudly asserts that he is self-supporting.

1771—Back in Spain, he is commissioned to do his first fresco, for the Church of Our Lady of the Pillar in Saragossa.

1773—Marries Josefa Bayeu, sister of the painter Francisco, his teacher in Madrid.

1774—Mengs hires him to design cartoons for the Royal Tapestry Factory.

1779—Is received at the Court of Charles III.

1783—Portrait of *Count Floridablanca*, in which the artist depicts himself humbly presenting a painting to the minister.

1784—Birth of his son Xavier, the only one of five to survive.

1785—Appointed vice-director of the painting department at the Academy of San Fernando.

1789—Charles IV becomes King of Spain. Portrait of the *Osuna Family*.

1790—Elected member of the Academy of San Carlos in Valencia.

1791—Last four cartoons for tapestry, including the *Blind Fly* and *El Pelele*.

1792—First attack of the illness that is eventually to leave him deaf.

1793—Begins a series of aquatints, the *Caprichos;* draws pictures of the Inquisition, bullfighting and carnivals while convalescing in Andalusia.

1794—Portrait of *La Tirana*.

1795—Death of Bayeu. Appointed director of the painting department of the Academy of San Fernando. Portrait of the *Duchess of Alba*.

1797—Another portrait of the *Duchess of Alba*.

1798—Frescoes in the Church of San Antonio de la Florida in Madrid.

1799—Appointed First Painter of the Court. Begins publication of the *Caprichos*.

1800—Portraits of the *Countess of Chinchon*, Godoy's wife, and of the *Family of Charles IV*. The *Naked Maja* and the *Clothed Maja* are also done at about this time. (The *Naked Maja* is the second nude, the first being Velásquez's *Venus*, in the history of Spanish painting.)

1802—July 23: death of the Duchess of Alba, aged 40.

1803—Goya donates the plates of the *Caprichos* to Charles IV in order to protect himself from the Inquisition.

1807—Portrait of Godoy in a general's uniform.

1808—March 23: Murat, leading one of Napoleon's armies, enters Madrid. Charles IV abdicates. Goya is in Saragossa, a spectator during the city's resistance to the French, which he records in paint. Some of these paintings, found by the French in the studio of Palafox in 1809, are destroyed.

1810—Works on the prints of the 82 etchings, the *Disasters of War*, begun in 1808.

1811—*Majas on a Balcony*.

1811–12—Winter: widespread deaths brought on by starvation and cold; Goya nonetheless continues to work and collects material for the *Disasters of War*.

1812—Death of his wife, Josefa. Portrait of Wellington.

1814—Ferdinand VII returns to Madrid. Goya paints *Executions of May Second* and *May Third*. Devotes his time to working on the 33 plates of the *Tauromaquia*, which will earn him the popular nickname "Francisco of the Bulls."

1815—Self-portrait.

1817–18—Beginning of the *Disparates* series.

1819—Acquires the Quinta del Sordo and, after another attack of his illness, starts the "Black Paintings" on the walls of his house.

1823—The armies of the Holy Alliance, under the command of the Duc d'Angoulême, restore absolutism in Spain.

1824—Goya hides in the house of a priest, Don José de Duaso y Latre, and paints the portrait of his protector and of some of the members of his family. May 30: is allowed to go to France. September: settles in Bordeaux. Visits the Salon in Paris, which is celebrating the triumph of the Romanticism of Delacroix. Lithographs, the *Bordeaux Bulls*.

1826—Back in Madrid, resigns as court painter and receives a pension. Vicente Lopez paints his portrait.

1827—Another trip to Madrid. Portrait of his small grandson *Mariano;* paints the *Bordeaux Milkmaid*. Returns to Bordeaux with Mariano.

1828—Unfinished portrait of José Pio de Molina. Dies on April 16.